Glacier and Waterton Lakes National Parks

A Postcard Book

FALCON™

D1457819

Design, typesetting, and other composition work by Falcon Press® Publishing Co., Inc., Helena, Montana. Printed in Korea.

ISBN 1-56044-323-5

Falcon Press publishes a wide variety of books and calendars. For a free catalog write Falcon Press, P.O. Box 1718, Helena, Montana 59624, or call toll-free 1-800-582-2665.

Front cover: Glacier National Park, Reynolds Creek below Reynolds Mountain

These slightly oversized postcards require first-class postage.

Glacier National Park

Reynolds Creek drains the slopes of 9,125-foot Mount Reynolds, the prominent horn peak directly south of the visitor center at Logan Pass.

Glacier National Park

First light adds a palette of pastel colors to a fall morning on 9,642-foot
Going-to-the-Sun Mountain.

Glacier National Park

Small waterfalls and water-loving plants decorate the paths of many creeks
and streams in Glacier. Peak runoff in the park usually occurs in mid-June.

Glacier National Park

Glacier is home to the grizzly bear, and the presence of this remarkable
animal makes the park a special place. It is estimated
that 200 grizzlies live in and near the park.

Waterton Lakes National Park

Bison grazing the prairie in Waterton. Recently, Waterton–Glacier
International Peace Park was included in the international program
of Biosphere Reserves to safeguard its ecosystems.

Glacier National Park

A light coating of snow brings the first touch of winter to the shoreline
of Lake McDonald and the summits of surrounding mountains.

Glacier National Park

Lush foliage and colorful wildflowers thrive along the Garden Wall on the
west side of Logan Pass. Towering above the pass on the east side,
Mount Reynolds catches the last rays of sun.

Glacier National Park

From June to September as many as 200 species of wildflowers blanket the slopes of Glacier. Glacier lilies, like this one, appear in early summer.

Glacier National Park

Only a black bill and black eye interrupt the solid white of a white-tailed
ptarmigan's winter plumage, a stark contrast to its mottled brown,
gray, and white plumage in summer.

Glacier National Park

Red monkeyflowers, like other alpine plants, are well adapted for surviving
and reproducing during the brief summers at Glacier.

Glacier National Park

Snow-capped peaks crown the autumn splendor of the Garden Wall.
The park's soaring mountains inspired early visitors to call
Glacier the "Crown of the Continent."

Glacier National Park

Rocky Mountain bighorn sheep, once rare at Logan Pass, are now seen
frequently in the moraines near Clements Mountain.

Galcier National Park

A field of sticky arnica, alpine daisy, Indian paintbrush, and other wildflowers covers the slopes below Mount Rockwell.

PHOTO BY MICHAEL S. SAMPLE

Glacier National Park

A lone glacier lily blooms near a stream below Clements Mountain on the
Continental Divide. These waters will continue to flow eastward and
eventually spill into Hudson Bay.

Glacier National Park

Blanketflowers and lupines decorate Apikuni Flat below the rugged face
of Apikuni Mountain near Lake Sherburne.

PHOTO BY MICHAEL S. SAMPLE

Waterton Lakes National Park

Together, Glacier National Park in Montana and Waterton Lakes National Park in Alberta form Waterton–Glacier International Peace Park.

Glacier National Park

In the high country of Glacier, wildflowers such as this Indian paintbrush
reach peak bloom in late July.

Glacier National Park

On a calm day in the Many Glacier area, beautiful Lake Josephine reflects Grinnell Glacier and 9,553-foot Mount Gould.

Glacier National Park

The drive to Many Glacier Hotel is particularly delightful in spring and
summer, when wild flowers flourish in the valley between
the Swiftcurrent and Boulder ridges.

Glacier National Park

Mountain goats are a favorite attraction to Glacier Park visitors. Goat kids
are born in May or June; about one birth in forty produces twins.

Glacier National Park

Beargrass, the unofficial park flower of Glacier, lines the trail to Iceberg
Lake. The name is misleading, since beargrass is a lily, and not a grass.

Waterton Lakes National Park

Sunrise where the prairie meets the mountains. The jagged peaks of
Waterton rim the cold, deep lakes that form the nucleus of the park.

MONTANA ADVENTURES

Explore the rest of the Glacier area with
these books. They'll lead you to
safe and memorable adventures.
For more information on
outdoor guides, nature books,
and unique western gift ideas,
call toll-free or complete this
card and return it to Falcon.

1-800-582-2665

Name:_____

Address:_____

City, State, Zip:_____

Phone:_____

FALCON™
P.O. BOX 1718
HELENA, MT 59624

FALCON™

BUSINESS REPLY MAIL
FIRST-CLASS MAIL PERMIT NO 80 HELENA MT

POSTAGE WILL BE PAID BY ADDRESSEE

FALCON™
PO BOX 1718
HELENA MT 59624-9948